THE BLAC SURVIVAL GUIDE

TEN STEPS FOR SURVIVING AS A BLACK UNITARIAN UNIVERSALIST AND HOW ALLIES CAN KEEP IT 100

REV. XOLANI KACELA, PH.D.

The Black UU Survival Guide:
Ten Steps for Surviving as a Black Unitarian Universalist
and How Allies Can Keep It 100

Rev. Xolani Kacela, Ph.D.

Illustration by Kimber McLaughlin

ISBN: 9781513667256

xk@revdrxk.com
www.revdrxk.com

Any questions? Tweet me: @xolanikacela

I dedicate this book to my dear friend, the Rev. Hope Johnson, who dedicated much of her life to helping Black people survive and thrive in Unitarian Universalism.

I dedicate it to Black people finding their way in Unitarian Universalism.

I dedicate it to all UUs dismantling white supremacy culture and authentically supporting Black UUs.

CONTENTS

Advance Praise i

Foreword v

Introduction vii

About You 1

    ABOUT YOU (Alternative for Aspiring Allies) 3

About Me 5

About This Guide 9

Acknowledgements 11

The Ten Steps 13

Step One 15

    What is Unitarian Universalism? 15

    Respect For and Openness To All people 16

Step Two 19

    Being New and Black 19

    Accepting Nostalgic Feelings 21

    Navigating Other Cultural Differences 21

    Leaving Familiar Sunday faces 22

    Embracing a Focus on Social Justice 23

    Be As Authentic As You Can 23

    Why We Love UUism 24

CONTENTS

Step Three **25**

How To Find Your Place 26

Read Your Church's Newsletter 26

Read UUA Publications 26

Go To A Board Meeting. 27

Understand How UU Churches 28

Raise and Spend Money 28

A Word About Covenants. 29

Creating Covenantal Community. 30

Step Four **31**

Fellow Black UUs May Not
See Things As You Do. 33

You Only Represent Yourself, ...33

Not All Black People/UUs 33

Develop Your Skills In 34

Non-Violent Communications 34

Help Others Develop Necessary Skills 35

Other -isms. 35

Another Word About Covenants. 36

Step Five. **37**

A Personal Example .37

CONTENTS

Write Out Your Core Convictions About Faith . . . 40

Jot Down Your Own Theology 40

Your Personal Mission Statement 41

Learn To Relate With
Non–UU Family and Friends 41

Expect To Lose Family and Friends 43

Expect To Gain Spiritual, ... 44

Intellectual, and Social Freedom 44

Joining a Long Tradition of Black Free Thought . . 45

Step Six **47**

BLUU 47

DRUUMM 48

Finding Our Way Home 49

Centering: Navigating Race, Authenticity,
and Power in Ministry, Mitra Rahnema, Editor . . 49

*Widening the Circle of Concern: Report of the UUA
Commission on Institutional Change, June 2020.* 50

Step Seven **51**

Learn Good Listening and Respond Accordingly . . 52

Step Eight **53**

What is Polity? 54

CONTENTS

Step Nine **57**

Learn About the UUA and Its Mission 57

Volunteer Positions on Committees 57

What Is General Assembly?. 58

What Happens There?. 58

Scholarship Funds for BIPOCs 58

Do Some Networking 58

Get Charged Up for Your Local Congregation 59

Considering Becoming a Religious Professional?. .59

Step Ten **61**

Practical Matters .61

Ministering While Black. 63

White Colleagues May Not Understand 63

Black Preaching or Other Differences. 63

White and Black Clergy Collegiality. 64

FOR ALLIES (INCLUDING CLERGY): 65

UU Clergy Are Not Trained In
Supervision and Conflict Resolution. 66

There Are Very Few Clergy Invitations To Preach .67

A Parting Caveat 68

ADVANCE PRAISE

This is a hopeful time to be a Unitarian Universalist of Color. The UU commitment to dismantle the culture of white supremacy within the faith and to work against the persistence of that culture in the world seems real. Yet it is true that many Black UU's still need a *Survival Guide.*

Commitment to a religious community that knows it remains a work in process around race does require survival skills. And some support. *The Survival Guide* offers both. Xolani's personal stories will strike familiar chords for many BIPOC UU's and acknowledging the particular challenges we face can be a comfort. White allies can also gain additional insight into the journey many Black UU's are making.

Perhaps the greatest gift of the *Survival Guide* is that it is a story of survival, of the successful religious transformation Xolani has lived and the place he has found in Unitarian Universalism. The Black UU story is as varied as the Black community. In Unitarian Universalism we need more narratives of survival if this liberal faith is itself to be transformed.

–Rev. Bill Sinkford
Senior Minister, First Unitarian Church, Portland, OR
First Black President, Unitarian Universalist Association

Reverend Xolani Kacela's ("Rev. XK") book, *The Black UU Survival Guide*, gives valuable witness to how folks who identify as BIPOC can and have experienced our Unitarian Universalist (UU) congregations. As a fierce anti-racist and aspiring ally, his experience gives me great pause. This book provides a much-needed blueprint and can be a useful tool for those of us who identify as European American (or white) in providing more support to current and future BIPOC ministers and congregants going forward. Furthermore, we can learn about our own behavior and how to be better ancestors and partners in this beloved faith of ours. I am grateful to Rev XK's heart work and emotional labor in putting pen to paper as he recounts his direct and often troubling experience. If you identify as a white UU, I urge you to breathe deeply as you read and take it in, no matter how disturbing it is to hear this truth. You may not have heard any of this before as many BIPOC will not share deeply if they do not feel it is safe to do so. This is a gift he has given us. I highly suggest we hear it as such. Rev XK deserves our deep and abiding gratitude.

While, as he states several times in this publication that he is speaking from his direct experience, we would be doing him and other BIPOC ministers and congregants a huge disservice to dismiss his observations as only one example. In my 20+ years of experience with multiple UU congregations and as the European American wife of a Black UU minister, I can tell you, the examples are similar to the experience of many BIPOCs in our association. I have seen it personally and I have heard it from my BIPOC or antiracist European American friends who serve the UUA. Perhaps what resonates most for me is that Rev XK's experience is so similar to what my husband, who has served this association proudly for over 25 years as a BIPOC minister, has shared with me that I am excited for him to shed light so we can all see it clearly. My hope (and recommendation) is this book becomes a resource to bring us together as one faith community and share our fully expressed selves with one another in a life-affirming way, referred to by some as Collective Liberation. May it be so.

–Lisa Stiffler-Bailey, Unitarian Universalist Congregation of Las Vegas, NV

I wish this book/road map had been available when I returned to UU church as an adult. Like many raised in this tradition I stopped going to church after high school and returned when I became a parent. It was fatiguing to be constantly treated like I was new member and new to the tradition even after 15 years at the same church. The navigational wisdom of Rev. Xolani Kacela and *The Black UU Survival Guide* is long overdue. With very practical tactics and engaging stories, Rev. Kacela provides useful tools and tactics for navigating the cultural minefield of microaggressions and the almost constant winds of othering faced when BIPOC folks walk into our mostly white churches. If you are white this book provides instructive, and for some sobering, reminders for how to better create a culture of belonging for all."

–Jesse King, first Black Chair of the UUA Ministerial Fellowship Committee

Sincerely this is a great book. It is a very smooth read, educational and straightforward without a lot of overwhelmingly "big words." I would have appreciated reading this, more than *A Chosen Faith*, when I first started learning more about Unitarian Universalism.

I found myself nodding and saying "Amen" more than once when reading. Navigating Cultural Differences in Step 2 was spot on for me.

I'm very thankful to have been raised on gospel music. I do not necessarily agree with the teachings of the church I grew up in, but it does always feel like "going home" when I'm there. It can be hard to let go of what you consider "standards of church," so the reassurance to do so is comforting.

I also valued the step to Be As Authentic As You Can Be! I looked around at the Zoom squares and really understood that I was the only person in that space who didn't look like anybody else. It feels like a gift, and/or a responsibility to be my authentic self, especially in spaces where I'm the only one bringing these perspectives and experiences to the table.

The last message to allies is my favorite; powerful, and so important.

–Kellie Ingram
BIPOC Director of Religious Education, UU Church of Las Cruces

FOREWORD

R ev. Kacela has gifted us with this gem of a powerful telling of his truth. He has taken care to remind us that as Black UUs, each of us has our unique experience of entry into the faith. He moves us through the arc of celebrating "a new find," a UU congregation with values that we hold dear. He invites us to consider how we might engage in this community and this faith – as member, minister, religious professional, and beyond. He reminds us that, indeed, "we are our ancestors wildest dreams." This includes being fully UU. While celebrating our beloved faith, he has taken care to draw attention to the many less than stellar experiences that Blacks continue to share in white supremacy-based places of worship and of faith.

As if that were not enough, Rev. Kacela invites white UUs who yearn for racial wholeness into the conversation to listen keenly, understand, and not question what Black UUs experience. He invites them to be emboldened to appropriately embrace authentic accompaniment of Black UUs. Rather than calling you out, Rev. Kacela is calling you in to a union, described by activist Brittany Packnett,[1] *"that allows power to be informed by love and disrupt all that stands in the way of freedom."* She asserted, *"I am calling you in to family and beloved community with one another."*

1 *UUA Ware Lecturer, 2018*

I believe that there is a force greater than ourselves, telling us that we need to ensure belonging Black, BIPOC communities, and whites. We know, instinctively, how to be caring siblings. But we humans are very good at resisting our instincts, especially when they're telling us to do something that takes us out our comfort zone. If you're human, you pretty much hear the call to connection. But hearing and responding are two very different things.

This courageous book engages the spirit of Sankofa, as the Ghanaian Sankofa bird, who is taking the time to look back, with the egg of the future in her mouth. If you are wondering what is hatching in the egg that the Sankofa bird holds in its mouth, notice that you are holding this book.

It is our Sankofa egg that will encourage us to be better UUs in communities in which we all truly belong. As I look back, I note that this call has been voiced for many years. We are now seeing benefits of staying true to the call for welcome equity centered in Black U community.

My twin sister, the late Rev. Dr. Hope Johnson always celebrated Rev. Dr. Xolani Kacela's ministry of care, courage, challenge, and call. In a biblical sense, Rev. Xolani heeded the call, "Whom shall I send, and who shall go for me?" He responded by saying, Here I am, send me!" This powerful book is an answer to his call. For this, I give thanks.

Dr. Janice Marie Johnson, Co-Director of Ministries and Faith Development, UUA

INTRODUCTION

ABOUT YOU

Y ou're a Black person looking for a new place to worship. You found your way to a Unitarian Universalist (UU) congregation, and the worship style inspired you in unexpected ways. You didn't know "spiritual, but not religious" churches were a thing. Perhaps the UU principles caught your attention; they seem thought-out and you've seen nothing like them in other churches. You think you may have discovered that church home you've been looking for.

It could be you visited a UU church just one time and wish you knew more. Or maybe you've been a few times, or more than a few. Most likely, your status is still "visitor," even if you've been attending a while. (In fact, the low-key approach to member recruitment seems odd to you. Did you miss "the ask"? You're used to Black churches extending the "right hand of fellowship" on the very first visit! Is this just how they do things here, you wonder, or could it be because you're Black?)

You notice you are the only, or one of very few Black, Indigenous and other People of Color (BIPOC) at services. You're wondering why Black people aren't attending the church. The people you have met here have been welcoming, but you feel a little lonely. You realize most of your friends

1

and family would not gravitate toward a majority-white church—and even if they did, you're not sure they'd feel as comfortable as you are in this setting.

There's a chance you haven't told your family and friends about your discovery. You're aware UUs talk a lot about liberal religion, gay marriage, women preaching, and the "all people have inherent worth" thing. Though these convictions mesh well with your values, those close to you may think you have gone off the deep end. They think you've turned your back on your religious upbringing. Your family may think you've given up your home training.

You may be the odd person out amongst your peers because you abandoned religious teachings from your past life, in part or whole. You gave them up when your experience pointed you down a different path. Attending the UU church feels like it is helping you regain some of your footing. You felt right at home listening to the sermons. You noticed—and didn't mind—that the minister either didn't read scripture or read offerings from multiple traditions.

Perhaps you have begun attending church routinely on Sundays and recognize people's faces here and there. You know a few people's names. Folks have been friendly ... yet none of them have offered to sit with you on Sundays or invited you to get together beyond the church services and coffee & fellowship hour.

You are unsure how to get more involved because no one has cornered you to explain. You are unsure what it will feel like to engage further in a community with so few BIPOCs. You long for fellowship that includes other Black "spiritual but not religious" types like you, people open to non-traditional gender identities, and other progressive perspectives, but this is the community you have found, and despite its limitations, it has unique attractions for you.

What's next?

ABOUT YOU (Alternative for Aspiring Allies)

You're a white member of a UU church. You are delighted to see Black, Indigenous, and other People of Color (BIPOC) show up occasionally in the pews on Sunday and wonder why so few stick around. You may have brought this up in membership meetings or puzzled over it with friends. You may have tried to invite a BIPOC or two to try out a service. This guide is for you, too (but in a supporting role kind of way).

The target audience here are Black UUs or prospective Black UUs, and it is written by a Black UU minister. If you are truly intentional about being a white ally, use this material to gain insight into how some Black UUs experience our UU church communities. That said, there is no monolithic population of Black UUs; we are all different. But with few exceptions, Black UUs are a small caucus in all UU churches. We tend to be regarded differently than white UUs. And our voices often get marginalized. So listen closely and take it seriously.

I hope you will accept the mostly implicit (and some explicit) advice on how you as an ally can keep it 100. *"Keeping it 100"* is another way of saying keeping it real or "honoring your own experiences and feelings. Keeping it 100 invites you to be honest by prioritizing your truth. Each of us needs to separate our own truth from our parents, spouses/partners, friends, communities, and culture. As related to being an ally, it means choosing to act in alignment with your express desires.

For example, if you believe there needs to be more equity and inclusion among White and BIPOC UUs, you'll need to act in ways that makes such equity and inclusion a reality. Your new way of being may include sacrifices you hadn't previously considered. You may need to give up some of your privilege, preferences, and power so that BIPOC UU can exert more of their own, instead. Be prepared to abandon, or revise, the "truths" you learned about earlier

3

in life about BIPOCs that led to contemporary disparities in UU culture.

It also means taking responsibility for your lack of understanding about race, racism, and the lives of BIPOCs. Be open and curious about how you developed the perspectives you have. What experiences do you draw upon when forming your views and ways of relating to and understanding BIPOCs.

This work of supporting Black UUs (you can call it practicing anti-racism or dismantling white supremacy culture within) requires an intentional effort to be in right relationship with Black UU clergy and laity. White allies need to find their way to acting authentically—the way they generally, or ideally, act with one another—when they are around and in relationship with BIPOCs. You'd think that would be easy, but evidence suggests it is not. I am hoping this book may help.

Caveat: "Ally" is not a title to claim or to self-identify as. I view the term as something whites might aspire to be. Once you self-proclaim yourself as an "ally," you are likely to lose street cred. On the other hand, I appreciate any person who boldly acts as an ally would in real-time. An example would be saying out loud someone said or acted in an offensive way toward a BIPOC individual. Such a shout out would visibly align the white supporter with the BIPOC individual in a way that models right relationship.

ABOUT ME

What's up, UUs! **I'm Xolani Kacela, or "xk."** **Here's the scoop on me.**

I am the minister at the UU Church of Las Cruces, NM; a chaplain with the New Mexico Air National Guard; member of the UUA Nominating Committee; author; spouse; and friend. Before these assignments, I was assistant minister at two large UU churches, and as an affiliate minister of another UU church. I have served as chair of the UUA Commission on Appraisal and as a member of the Ministerial Fellowship Committee (MFC).

I've taught Pastoral Ministry at Meadville-Lombard Theological School, one of the UU seminaries. I am a good officer in the UU Ministers Association. Good officers assist ministers navigating conflict and thorny issues in their ministries.

Before becoming a UU, I was ordained as clergy in the United Methodist Church (UMC) clergy. Long ago, I was a Baptist, and before that, I belonged to the African Methodist Episcopal Church (AME). I have visited dozens of other churches from many denominations along the way.

I started on my path to becoming UU clergy right in the middle of my UMC ordination process. I was about a year away from being conferred the rank of Elder with Full Connection in the United Methodist Church (North Texas Conference), and serving as a hospice chaplain at the time, when I visited a patient dying of breast cancer. She invited me to her house to discuss her spiritual life with the caveat, "I don't know if I believe in God." I accepted her invitation.

We enjoyed a warm conversation about death. It turned out she was a member of the First Unitarian Church of Dallas. I scoped the church's newsletter on her coffee table while she got me a glass of water.

The newsletter was professionally done and contained a lot of content about the church's activities. I recall thinking to myself, *"How do they do so much at that church?"* We discussed the congregation, and I made a mental "post it note" to look for the church when I had spare time. On another hospice visit a month later, I passed by the church and recognized the name. I visited the church one Sunday about a month later.

First Unitarian of Dallas looks like a traditional Christian church, large and cathedral-like, but with beautiful contemporary architecture. I was one among two or three other Black persons in the sanctuary that Sunday. The worship service was Christian in flow, but not in content. The ministers preached from scripture and other sources and were great messengers. Their messages inspired people but were not too preachy.

People welcomed me as I strolled through the coffee hour. I met the minister, who was also cordial. We exchanged information, and I joined the church some months later. Soon, I became a member of the staff!

My path in Unitarian Universalism has been fast, furious, and at times, infuriating. I've served four congregations, served on the district level, and on the national level. It's been an interesting ride. I've been through some highs and lows and come out (so far) in good enough shape to help you navigate your path as a UU.

Why not write for all BIPOCs (Black, Indigenous, and other People of Color)? you may ask. Though we BIPOCs have a lot in common, I can only write from my experience. I am a Black, heterosexual, married man. I prefer to write about what I know and not project my biases and prejudices on people with other identities.

I don't have all the answers. You may find that I have no answers. There are other Black UUs with more experience, power, and influence with UUism than I have. (But only I have written this Guide!)

This book arose from years of attending a popular retreat among religious professionals of color within the UUA, Finding Our Way Home (FOWH), breaking bread with Black religious professionals, and hearing and sharing stories and laments about the trials and tribulations we experience in our faith. When I attended the first retreat, the attendees included mostly UU clergy of color, LGBTQ+ UUs, and some allies. During that meeting, we broke into caucus groups and I recall hearing the many travails of my colleagues.

Still a staff member at First Unitarian of Dallas, which had supported me well, I was naïve about how bad things could get for clergy of color in the faith. As time passed, I faced some of those difficulties and learned how to navigate many, in part with the help of other leaders' wisdom and support—and now I hope to make the way easier for others coming up in the community.

ABOUT THIS GUIDE

This book is for you if you are Black and fall into one or more of these categories: (1) you are new to Unitarian Universalism, (2) you find yourself disconnected in a congregation, (3) you have run into conflict, (4) you find it difficult understanding what UUism is really about, and/or (5) you find yourself contemplating UU ministry. Together, we'll explore such topics as joining a UU church, identifying yourself as UU, navigating UU culture (including well-meaning white folks and systems of white supremacy; and even finding job opportunities within the association.

The hidden agenda is getting you to become a permanent fixture in the faith.

I've based this content on my personal experience. You'll discover my biases in this work. This book is not a comprehensive work. It doesn't portend to have all the answers. And another Black UU minister or layperson may indeed offer you another perspective. Where possible, I'll provide links to other content and resources.

This survival guide has one purpose: to help you become the best UU you can be. I believe that if you have insider information about the UU faith that helps you navigate these particular waters, you're more likely to stay with it, enjoy your experience, and even help grow our numbers among other Black persons of faith.

One of my early UU mentors, the Rev. Dr. Laurel Hallman, informed me that entering UU ministry meant I needed time to learn the "UU style." I'm still learning (and nudging that style in new directions) fifteen years later! This small book is an attempt to share some of my learnings with you so that you might avoid some traps that often short-circuit Black people in the faith. I want to provide resources and some sense-making which validates your experiences and serves as breadcrumbs along the way.

I will share with you tricks and traps associated with being a UU as a Black person. My purpose with this book is not to name names and single out individual people, but I do hope to highlight systems and structures within the Unitarian Universalist Association and UU congregational ministries that Black UUs will benefit from knowing about when making decisions regarding membership and engaging the faith.

This is an independent effort, and does not reflect the views of the UUA, its entities or affiliates. I didn't collaborate with nor seek endorsement from organizations promoting UUism among Black people (though I am grateful for feedback from many peers who graciously previewed it with a critical eye).

ACKNOWLEDGEMENTS

I am grateful to UUA leaders such as our UUA President, the Rev. Susan Frederick-Gray, who has made dismantling white supremacy culture and the Black Lives Matter movement centerpieces of her administration's work. She has moved the UUA in the right direction.

I have deep gratitude for other great UUs: Taquiena Boston, Dr. Janice Marie Johnson, Rev. Keith Kron, Rev. Richard Nugent, Rev. Sarah Lammert, Jesse King, and others. Each of them has illuminated the struggles of religious professionals of color, taken seriously our concerns, and made conditions better. I'm also grateful for my Black colleagues who support me and allow me to support them as they serve.

THE TEN STEPS

STEP ONE

GETTING TO KNOW THE BASICS

What is Unitarian Universalism?

I consider Unitarian Universalism as one of the Divine's love and transformation agents in the world. That is XK's definition. It comes from my heart and experience. You won't find it in textbooks or a hymnal.

The short history of the faith is this: Unitarian Universalism united two uniquely American religious movements that developed out of and diverged from other forms of Protestantism. The Unitarians viewed God as a single being. Their theology contained no "Father, Son, and Holy Spirit." They believed in the oneness of God. The church emphasized both God's love and human free will. The Universalists believed in God's unrelenting love to save all souls. They believed nothing a human being could do would turn off God's love. They argued God would never banish a person to darkness based on sin or beliefs. The church emphasized the embrace of those who were otherwise marginalized in society. Among the flagship church's charter members was a freed, formerly enslaved person, and the denomination was the first to ordain women.

These two churches became one in 1961 and named themselves Unitarian Universalism (UU). The UU Association (UUA) now has affiliated congregations around the world. Members (and fellow travelers) of those UU communities are known as UUs.

I classify UUism within Protestantism, which is to say that we have Protestant origins, sources, and in many churches, similar liturgy or order of service. There are many practicing and former Christians in UU churches. You'll discover that UU Christians will vary in belief from person to person. Many UU churches have a Christian group and there is a UU Christian Fellowship that meets at General Assembly, the annual UU denominational meeting, and during the year at neutral sites.

But it is hard to ignore that UU beliefs are different from those of other faiths or denominations you have experienced. The reality is that while UUism has its origins in Christianity, and specifically American Protestantism, UUism draws people from any number of backgrounds, and many understandings of God—including those who do not hold a belief in a traditional notion of God, are skeptics, or are atheists. There are many UUs who consider themselves humanists or "spiritual, but not religious." There are also UUs who consider themselves Christian or who align with other faiths while finding fellowship in UUism.

Respect For and Openness To All people

UUism is a religious faith without religious doctrine or dogma. UU churches develop their missions according to seven shared UU principles. They create covenants for treating people with respect. UU churches and clergy very consciously lift up the wisdom of many different faith traditions and, also in the name of (small-u) universalism, have long strived to be inclusive. UUs were among the first churches to actively welcome LGBTQ+ parishioners, for instance, and to ordain gay and lesbian ministers.

The UU Principles attract many people. For some, they represent the first encounter with such ideas in religious materials. Marginalized people become overjoyed and experience comfort reading the first principle, "the inherent worth and dignity of every person." They feel they've hit the spiritual jackpot. Equality is a driving force in the UU world.

Such inclusion extends to all people. UUs welcome all people, of every ethnicity, race, sexual orientation, gender identity or expression, age, class, and religious background, among other ways people self-identify or register with others. That's a unique attribute UUs should brag about. You'll discover UUs striving to live out their welcome with genuine hospitality and respect.

STEP TWO

KEEPING AN OPEN MIND

Survival begins by adjusting your expectations for UU congregational life. You will be leaving many expectations at the door. Ready?

Being New and Black

UU congregations are friendly, progressive, often politically active, open and welcoming, and predominantly white. If the demographics of a UU congregation yield 10% people of color, that is a high level of racial diversity. The UUA does not keep racial demographic records, so there is no accurate number of Black members in the denomination. You may be the only Black person in the pews, or one of very few. But being in the minority is a fact of many aspects of Black life, beyond UUism. We do this day in, day out. The UU church just needs to prove worth it for us to do with our Sundays.

Don't expect people to see you through a lens, darkly, nor through rose-colored glasses. While they may want to ignore your Blackness, they won't, can't, and truly, shouldn't. Hopefully, they can keep it 100.[2] Most won't realize they view you through a racial lens, or through racism, but that is how they very well may treat you.

Truthfully, UU congregational consultants often report

2 Keeping it 100 is a new phrase that means keeping it real or being authentic.

UU congregants are conflict-avoidant and in denial about racism[3], as are many white people. They may become defensive if you bring up race. Ridding yourself of this expectation that white UUs really know what they are doing when it comes to being anti-racist[4] will improve your survivability. (Some do and will surprise you, but to quote poet and author Alice Walker, let's "live frugally on surprise"!)

Here's the good news. Most UUs welcome you to the congregation with genuine care. They will extend you a warm welcome during the service, after the service, and throughout coffee hour. People will smile and extend their hands to you sincerely. It's up to you, to some extent, what happens next.

Some folks may be courteous but keep at arm's length when they meet you for the first time. They're trying to check you out and do the church thing of being friendly. You should feel wary when people approach you too enthusiastically, aggressively, or without boundaries. Today's culture calls that "over sharing." They are likely not aware that your status as a racial minority in their midst is fueling their over-enthusiasm. Help them bring the energy down to a nice even keel if you're able. It truly is not unusual to meet people after services and get into a deep conversation if you hit it off.

Being sincere and down-to-earth opens the door to genuine rapport. Go for it if you feel comfortable. I know introverts will find this daunting. Give it your best shot, anyway. When you share your life with people, you open a door and encourage them to return the favor. We need more relating in UUism.

We also need more diversity. In most UU congregations, as noted at this chapter's outset, you'll be the only Black person or one of very few. You should get used to that. Or as you grow in the faith, become a good evangelist for UUism and

3 This research is borne out by an instrument known as the Intercultural Developmental Inventory that is given when congregations engage in anti-racism, anti-oppression, and multicultural work.
4 I define anti-racist as actively and consciously so, not passively "not racist."

bring your family and like-minded friends to join alongside you, if you think they'd be interested... and if they can make the transition.

Accepting Nostalgic Feelings

A funny thing happens when UUs of color gather at retreats or conferences. We find ourselves nostalgic for gospel-like elements of worship and begin singing the music we steered clear of on our way to becoming UUs. That music allows us to celebrate our Blackness in a safe space as it bubbles to the surface amid this UU context. The pop-up chorus is a subtle reminder of from whence we came. If we could have this in our home UU spaces, what a world it could be.

When I served in Durham, my colleague Sherman Logan, who serves at the UU church in Richmond, Virginia, preached for us. He came accompanied by his sister's gospel choir, which sang at two services. That choir blew the roof off the church and had the congregation on their feet swaying to the music. That service spoke to the power of interfaith work to transform people's hearts, minds, and perceptions of faith communities.

Know where your nostalgia comes from. I believe nostalgia starts with memories of satisfying Black church experiences that arise when Black UUs grow exhausted from bearing the pressures of being the only Black in a white church. The exhaustion triggers trauma responses for some. We all have trauma in our past. As our brains try to relieve that pain, we recall comforting memories. Without knowing it, we're longing for the good old days.

Navigating Other Cultural Differences

Just to make things more complicated, sometimes the music sounds the same, but it's the words that are different. Often UU hymnals will call on familiar melodies but change the words to better match most UUs' beliefs.

And then there's this. In UU spaces, people can show up too relaxed. UUs can act informally in services, and in meetings. This will put off Blacks accustomed to different behavior standards at church. In some UU churches, people speak out during worship as if they were at a picnic (while staying oddly silent during sermons). It's not the Black church way. The culture may defy what you're accustomed to as a Black person in a church. Such differences in worship style can interfere with a good UU message or worship.

The white supremacy that lurks in UU spaces, as it does in most majority-white spaces, leads white UUs to expect Black UU to just adapt to UU congregational culture and normalize it. Give yourself time to adjust, knowing white members generally don't mean harm. They have different approaches to church than what you know. But do resist their efforts, witting or unwitting, to make you adapt. Be a confident change agent and bring people along with you. Work with the minister or worship team to re-imagine the worship experience for a wider audience.

Leaving Familiar Sunday faces

Leaving the Black church, if that's where you're coming from, means leaving much of your social community behind. They will not follow you. That means you must be at peace, not seeing them on Sundays or at all. You must find novel ways to connect with them. Since the church may be the only place you see those friends, not going to your old church means "goodbye." It's painful dissolving important relations like that. Most Black people won't do it. You find spiritual freedom but lose your people. It also means you gain a sense of isolation until you meet and make new friends.

Here's the bottom line. Choosing to be a UU takes years as you establish your new identity. First, you decide you need a religious practice different from everyone else in your circle. Then you leave your family's religion and make UUism your new faith. The work of growing into your chosen faith is a gradual process. It took me years to arrive at such a stance and awareness.

Embracing a focus on social justice

There is a strong emphasis on social justice within UUism. UUs are generally forward-thinking people on social issues. We thrive by standing up for justice, and often, that means taking liberal stances (though there are also UUs with conservative positions). We need all views standing together, working out differences, and reaching decisions for wise social actions. Collective wisdom helps UUs live up to our principles and values.

In some UU churches, I will add, the emphasis on social justice seems to overshadow spirituality. Some UU churches lack any reputation for spiritual practice. This could discourage Black people from getting involved in the faith. To my mind, playing down UU religious origins reduces the church's chances of attracting new Black members. That's my bias.

Be As Authentic As You Can

It is best to be yourself in these white UU contextual spaces. You'll find diverse thoughts in UU churches and expect it to surface from time-to-time. You should prepare yourself so you can defend your positions with reason and a convincing argument. Love and compassion ought to guide you when expressing your point of view.

Answer this: "Who is the true you?" I pose this question because being in a new congregation (even a UU one) can cause people to change depending on the context. In one situation, you bring one part of yourself to an experience; and in another situation, you bring another part of yourself. You may find you don't know what part of your experience to bring to any situation.

I recall attending meetings and sensing something was off but didn't know whether to say anything. That was because I lacked the confidence to assert the part of me needed at that moment. I'm prone to speak forthrightly now because I know myself and what I bring to the room. I also trust my inner compass will lead me in the right direction for the desired impact.

Why We Love UUism

I love being with UUs, but know that UUs are not perfect. I am a work in progress. You are, too. We are all waiting on that part of ourselves to catch up with a higher consciousness.

Being a UU helps you grow in spirit and master challenges. UUism has something in common with other faith groups and spiritualities. It doesn't protect you from the world's problems. There's no safety from life's suffering. Spiritual aches and pains only go away by finding their causes, allowing time to pass, and engaging healing practices.

When I served my first UU parish, there was among the staff a slogan that was a spinoff of a saying attributed to Gandhi. In her book titled with that saying, Alice Walker identified fellow Black poet June Jordan as the writer who penned the line, "We are the ones we've been waiting for." That slogan represented the liberal mindset of staff and members—and both the mindset (given the demographics of the movement), and the misattribution, revealed the staff's own rooting in white supremacist culture.

I raise this example because many believe UU culture is a remedy for the world's pain. The world isn't sitting around waiting on UUs to show up. UU spiritual practice leans into areas of pain and suffering that other faiths disavow as their responsibility. That is a great strength, but not the be all end all.

STEP THREE

JOINING A COMMUNITY

If you are interested in joining a particular UU congregation, don't wait for someone to invite you. It may never happen. Though UUs are open and friendly to all comers, there is unlikely to be a "doors of the church are open" moment in UU churches. Maybe no right hand of fellowship, either. Some congregations prefer you to visit for months or years to ensure you understand them before joining.

You join a UU congregation by signing their membership book. Most times, a minister initials or certifies that you've signed the book. Some congregations have bylaws that specify membership terms. Check them out at the church you intend to join. Ask to join when you are ready.

Many UU congregations don't have visible means for you to join. If you aren't intentional about joining, you may never discover the procedure. Most congregations expect you to come to them. This disheartens me. It feels like an unwitting voter suppression move against people who would be excellent members of congregations needing to grow. Those congregations, in my judgment, suppress their membership by keeping the membership book out of sight.

Ask someone on the staff, such as the minister, administrator, or a member who deals with membership about how to join. Join as soon as you feel called. Make your move as soon as you make a mental commitment. Don't let people talk you out of it, insisting you need to visit for a period to be certain. That's how people act in social clubs. This is about following your conscience.

If you happen to be (as I was) a seminarian contemplating UU ministry, join your church soon. You need a concrete membership date, and the clock is ticking. Either way, joining a place shows that you are serious in your commitment to community. So, once you feel ready, I encourage you to make the leap.

How To Find Your Place

Before and after joining, it is important to build relationships in your new spiritual home. Try to make friends and connect with them between Sundays to develop a genuine connection within the congregation. If you don't feel making friends is a possibility, try to connect with a small group or covenant group that has consistent meetings. Create at least one meaningful relationship. You may need that lifeline down the road.

Read Your Church's Newsletter

Pay attention to your church's events beyond worship. Knowing what is going on during the week at church gives you the knowledge and choices. You may have no desire for participating, but that means you're opting out and lessening the chance of feeling like you're in-the-loop.

Read UUA Publications

You can stay abreast of UUA headlines by reading *UU World*. It's published two times a year. When you join a UU church, you'll receive the magazine from the national association. It contains content about UU ministry, politics, social justice, careers, religious education, and so forth. It has an interesting classifieds section.

I find the publication is filled with white writers and few people of color. The editors seem to have little taste for the style of Black authors and choose white correspondents. If you have talent, consider approaching them about writing as you get more involved in UUism. I for one would love to see your byline.

Many UUs who live remotely separated from physical UU churches belong to the Church of the Larger Fellowship (CLF). The CLF publishes *Quest for Meaning*. It too, in my judgment, caters to white UU writers. This a substantial loss because many voices of color go under-represented in this publication.

Go To A Board Meeting

The best way to understand how the church works is by attending a board meeting. The governing board of the church creates the bylaws and policies and oversees the minister. These meetings are generally open to everyone. By attending them, you learn how the church runs behind the scenes and you can provide input regarding decisions.

Get a copy of the bylaws, read through them, and you'll better understand how you can influence the congregation. Be present and prepared for the congregational vote. Know the agenda. Serve on the board of trustees or other committees. Work from the inside. It takes about a year or two to understand enough about the church's history and inner workings to join the board.

Whether you become a board member or attend board meetings to contribute from the sidelines, show up prepared. You need to read the agenda and other materials distributed before the meeting. You'll arrive informed and ready to speak about the subject. Don't wait until you arrive to absorb the information and formulate your thoughts. That is a time suck that no one can afford, and you will lose credibility, which you will need to be effective.

Congregations have committees other than the board. There are generally committees on leadership, worship, ministry, finance, and social justice to name a few. Decide where your gifts and your passion meet, then get involved.

Understand How UU Churches Raise and Spend Money

Once you join, people will expect you to make a financial pledge and commit to getting involved. UU churches create their budgets based on large annual pledges, gifts, and dues more than on weekly collection plate donations. During a stewardship campaign, also known as a pledge drive, people pledge an amount they will give during the year. The money from the pledge drive funds the ministry. Think of pledging as agreeing to support the ministry over the next year. If you're used to giving your church $100 monthly, just pledge $1200 and you'll be 100.

Understand the church budget. It differs from other denominations. It's important to know where the money comes from. Every congregation creates a budget based on its annual operating expenses. These include salaries for ministers and staff, program expenses, maintenance, and monies contributed to the larger UUA.

Often in UU congregations, people with wealth and means will fund a significant portion of the church's expenses. Many donors contribute to the congregation's endowment fund. These become restricted or reserved funds that get invested and used only under certain circumstances. Donors dictate the terms of how the church spends the proceeds.

Everything that you see taking place in a UU congregation comes from the members' generosity and rarely from outside grants. The larger UUA receives a small allocation of church receipts to support its work. As quiet as it's kept, church funding doesn't grow on trees.

UUs don't enjoy talking about money. If you came from a Black Baptist church, you're accustomed to hearing two sermons every Sunday — one on the scriptural message and one on money! You need to participate in the annual meeting. Don't miss the action. UUs differs from many Black churches where people give to the church weekly. It's good to know the process.

A Word About Covenants

Covenants lie at the heart of UUism. A covenant is an agreement the congregation creates that describes how people will be together. It's a guideline for how they treat each other and settle conflicts. A covenant is a roadmap of promises that helps the church accomplish its mission.

Get familiar with the covenant and conduct yourself according to its agreements. That's the best avenue to avoid conflict, and it's hard. Putting the covenant first means putting your personal ambitions second. People who put personal ambitions ahead of the church's needs cause things to fall apart. Respecting covenants empowers churches to accomplish their mission.

When covenants break down, policies should offer direction. Most churches have written policies. You can also consult the bylaws. If you still don't feel safe meeting with a person who has caused you harm[5], reach out to a UU congregational consultant for advice. Every UU church belongs to a district and region with people trained to step into a difficult situation. Use them, as necessary.

Talk with the person you have a conflict with and resolve your differences. Consult a neutral third-party if you cannot meet one-on-one. A neutral party is someone who can listen

5 The issue of "harm" is important. By harm, I mean the experience of being threatened, inappropriately touched (body, hair, etc.), silenced or spoken over, verbally assaulted, etc. I have personally experienced UUs gaslighting me, yelling at me, and questioning my judgment. I know ministerial colleagues who have been physically threatened by church members on the premises of the congregation they served. Harm can be emotional, physical, sexual, or otherwise defined.

objectively without taking sides and help you hear one another more clearly. Keep working the process until you feel heard and understood. Allow me to add this caveat. As a UU minister, I strive to live by love and compassion. I've done a lot of "formation" work en route to establishing ministerial competency. Still, I am not perfect by any stretch of the imagination and continue making errors along the way. When I do, I give it my best shot to acknowledge my part in a situation, apologize, make amends, and remain in right relationship with others as we move on to the next thing.

Creating Covenantal Community

This work of surviving and thriving is an ongoing process. Here is my philosophy of community: building a church community depends on members' willingness to share their lives honestly, which encourages reciprocity. Without mutual support, we can't serve each other when they need us. When we can't serve one another, we can't fulfill our call to care. That disrupts the community.

In pastoral care work, committees are often hobbled in their efforts because people do not speak up about important events that require others' help. Then they will complain that no one came to help them. The same applies to the UU community when you're new. You need to share of yourself and allow others to share of themselves with you in order for everyone to discern each other's sincerity and fit into the community.

Bottom line: membership in a congregation is a two-way street. It requires you to be your best, most authentic self, and it requires a community to be its best self and welcome you while helping you integrate into it as a whole person. Expect the best from UUs and assume good intentions. You will most often find the same goodwill extended to you.

STEP FOUR

DEALING WITH RACE, RACISM, AND OTHER ISMS

Most UU churches need Black people as members. Yet UUs conduct little outreach to Black people. UUs do not believe in evangelizing, door-knocking, or other efforts to recruit Black members. You'll discover UUs will welcome you, hope you return, and encourage your involvement.

The friendly welcome does not mean UUs understand multiculturalism. There are few ways for any of us to become competent in race relations. Almost none of us were born with skills dealing with other cultural styles. We somehow expect this from white UUs.

Here's the breaking news. White UUs are often unaware of their rude treatment toward non-white UUs. Good intentions often collide with disrespectful acts or words. Add in microaggressions and church life gets turbulent.

Here is a situation I experienced once as a UU minister. The experience is an outlier for me, but not among BIPOCs, and it is absolutely a part of my UU survival story. You may have experienced something like it.

One Saturday, I was on campus at the Eno River UU Fellowship in Durham, North Carolina, where I served as assistant minister. The church was closed; I was there retrieving something from my office. As I approached the building, I saw one of our members, whom I knew and knew me, peering inside the dark office space. I had said to her, "How are you doing? What are you up to?" She responded by asking me, "Are you the janitor here?" To which I said, "I'm Xolani. You were in my office a few days ago!"

Her inability to recognize me caught me by surprise, but her instinctual assumption that I was the custodian stunned me. It's one thing not to know me "out of context," as they call it. It's another to assume the Black guy at the mostly white UU church must be the cleaning man. She was embarrassed and apologized profusely. I forgave the misidentification situation, chalked it up to stereotyping, and put it behind me.

It's seldom I don't recognize a church member "out-of-context." I may not know their name immediately, but I recognize faces. My lived experience tells me that white people have something else going on in these situations that is unconsciously racialized. They don't see us as they would see other white people. There is a limited range of possibilities for what roles we serve in their lives, and beyond that, we don't exist. Though we can be right in their faces, sometimes we're invisible. It's doubly difficult for many to see us as equals or authority figures.

Many "woke" UUs do not fit this mold. They are conscious and respectful toward Black UUs as they are all people. But my experience at Eno River reveals undertones in UU culture and ministry. You can expect varieties of this problem being Black in majority white spaces.

In UU spaces, most white people strive to bring their best selves to the table and to be respectful to non-white people. These are the "good ones," as one of my favorite UUs from Eno River was fond of saying. But there are unfortunately white UUs whose best self—despite our "shared values"— will not be hospitable to a Black person. They will see no reason to extend courtesy to you; their frame of reference will render you invisible. Don't let them get you in a funk. For every abrasive UU, there are at least four kind UUs.

Fellow Black UUs May Not See Things As You Do

The following may come as a big surprise.

Black UUs are not homogeneous. We don't all think alike. There may be no unity among Black UUs within a single congregation. Some Black UUs don't consider themselves as Black the way you do! Some think of themselves as "colorblind" and ignore the race dynamic they create. They may not even speak to you. They are over it.

Some Black UUs distance themselves from discussions of race and color. I don't know why. Maybe you can tell me. I'd once emailed all the Black people in my congregation. Only one of a dozen responded.

You Only Represent Yourself, Not All Black People/UUs

No matter how you play it, you only represent yourself. You don't represent all Blacks or people of color in your congregation. And don't act like there is a Black group you're speaking for. My advice is to bring your best self to any situation and try to be thoughtful and genuine.

As a Black person in a meeting, people will listen to you (sometimes). At other times, you will deal with white supremacy culture that can't hear you. People will discount your experience, placing their own above yours.

People might take you sharing your Black experience in any conversational setting for granted, even if that's not your style. Know this expectation is out there. You may not want to speak about your specific experience as a Black person. Or you may desire to speak about it. It's a gift knowing where you stand and letting people know upfront.

As a minister, it's seldom that people ask me about my Black experience. Perhaps it is because I speak about it from the pulpit. As a layperson, you will probably encounter people who think they know what Black experience is about based on their readings, TV shows, friendships with co-workers, or their assumptions about Black life. When that happens, be ready with some pleasant responses that still clarify where they may be in error. In UU spaces, there is at least a shared ideal and value system to which all can be held to account—and racist behavior should indeed be called out.

Develop Your Skills In Non-Violent Communications

You can expect both rude conduct and plain naïve practices. For that reason, you need skills in compassionate communication. Such skills help you listen while minimizing anger. The book, *Crucial Conversations: Tools for Talking when Stakes are High*, can help you handle the conflict. (That's just one of my favorites; there are others out there, too.)

I am not suggesting that you, the Black person, must do all the personal work. I am encouraging a proactive stance, so when the racial rubber hits the road, you don't leave the community. Instead, you can engage people with skill and grace. The skills necessary for non-violent conversations and other communication take time to develop. The same skills you gain for navigating race in the UU world will help you in everyday life (and vice versa).

Accepting poor conduct or giving in to hostile action breaks your spirit. You develop resentment, anger, and may never speak to the culprit again. Then you quit the church. That cheats you out of spiritual practice—worship, community service, and belonging.

So do speak up. Some incidents might prompt a critical conversation between you and the other person involved. Create a safe (or brave) space for the encounter. That means agreeing on the issues and listening deeply to one another. Only attempt this if you feel confident the person and conversation won't cause either of you more harm. Staying open and not getting triggered requires control and skill.

If you know or expect your restraint and/or skill is in short supply during such encounters, it might be worthwhile postponing the conversation until you're in a better headspace or when someone you trust is available to be with you while meeting with the offender. Simple awareness helps to control your emotions when triggers show up.

Help Others Develop Necessary Skills

Encourage your congregational leaders to seek professional consultants on anti-racism, anti-white supremacy, and multiculturalism.

Experts train church leaders on breaking down white supremacy. They help UUs understand racism and their

part in creating a racist culture. I have trained with Tema Okum and Michelle Johnson, who are the best. They are skilled in UU culture.

Church consultants provide needed resources for UU leaders. Taking part in their workshops demands courage. Participants get into their personal and shared history that brings up the painful past. The training is essential if churches want to grow in cultural skills.

Other -isms

Racism is not the only -ism that Black UUs encounter. If you're not young, you may face ageism. If you are female you may face misogyny. If you're in the LGBTQ community, you may face homophobia or transphobia. If you're Christian, you will meet people who disdain Christianity and look down upon you. If you're a person with disabilities, you'll deal with ableism. The list is endless.

You must quickly handle any disparate treatment thrown your way using the same courage described above. When you witness others in need of help, be their advocate. Don't be a bystander. UUs try abiding by the first principle of inherent worth, but none of us lives it out perfectly. Being proactive and advocating for -ismed (oppressed, minoritized, traditionally marginalized) people is one way that Black UUs help UUism reach its potential. This step is about connecting you with people. You want to build as many quality relationships with other UUs as you can. You must scour the surface for people willing to be in right relationship with you. This is the work you must do for yourself.

Another Word About Covenants

You *will* feel misunderstood or mistreated if you stay around long enough. Your first move should be to consult the covenant. Ask yourself if you are abiding by it. If not, get to it. If you are in covenant, determine whether the other party is. When they are out of covenant, try calling them back into covenant. That is a process of deep conversation, truth-telling, and reconciliation. A good covenant spells out how to hold people accountable. It also emphasizes relationships, not rules. I believe the most important elements are love and compassion. But bottom line: don't let people run you out of the church through coercion, bullying, racism, or other unfair means. When you are a member, the church belongs to you as much as it belongs to anyone else.

The church's history and work around anti-racism—as it relates to covenant and beyond—is a good indicator of its culture. We've worked at improving multicultural competency for decades within the faith. We still have a long road ahead.

STEP FIVE

KNOWING YOUR FAITH
CONVICTIONS, VALUES, AND BELIEFS

In becoming a UU, it is not enough settling with what you no longer believe. You'll only get into conflict and unwinnable arguments with people. Write and recite what you hold as your spiritual truths.

I've found myself in enough arguments about "truth" to know the best way to avoid them. They're set off by triggers. UUs who are former Christians get triggered by God-language, hymns, and prayer. It's normal to avoid these triggers in the UU world without resolving their cause. I believe it's better for you to expose the cause of your triggers and get a hold of why you are so reactive. Then find secular replacements to soothe your spirit. Gaps between your beliefs and your ability to articulate those beliefs expose you to triggers, anger, and isolation.

A Personal Example

This is how I've worked through my changing theological perspective. My path is not unlike many UUs who switched from one faith to Unitarian Universalism. I realized I was going through a change, a metamorphosis. Out of necessity, I had to come to grips with my inner turmoil as a Christian minister. Going from United Methodist to UU took me approximately two to three years of theological discovery.

Side note: We use the word "orthodoxy" when talking about belief. UUs don't speak of orthodoxy because of our openness to many belief systems. We lean more heavily on "orthopraxy," which refers to correct action.

The first thing that triggered my doubt about Christian doctrine was unrelated to religion. I was reading the book *The Fear of Flying* by Erica Jong during a flight to Europe. The book's main character glibly commented that religion was the stuff of quacks. It made me laugh, but it also triggered a curiosity pause. I immediately asked myself, could religion be quackery?

I consider that episode as my "crack in the shell" moment. Before that, I hadn't allowed myself to question my beliefs. First off, that would have been heretical. Second, questioning your beliefs means questioning your identity and your worldview. Who wants to see their identity under such scrutiny?

Such an exercise meant casting doubt over a lifetime of teaching by my family, Sunday school teachers, and broader friendship circle. It also meant questioning my training as a Christian minister. Putting that on the line might have jeopardized my career! You can see why people don't pursue these questions. The answers might lead you down a path you're not quite prepared to travel.

I concluded religion wasn't "quackery." Yet many beliefs I held before needed revision. Among the questions I asked myself were:

What is the meaning of "sin"?

How does sin play into the human condition?

What is the meaning of Jesus' life?

Who is God? Is there a God?

Do I need redemption and salvation?

What happens after death?

What is scripture and who gets to write it?

How does baptism work in my life?

What rites should be considered the sacraments (bread and wine)?

Is there a heaven and hell?

This questioning and revisioning process of my beliefs took time as I mulled over these concepts and rigorously tested their meanings.

I furthered my thinking by reading books from authors like Christopher Hitchens and Richard Dawkins. Both were nonbelievers and staunch atheists. Their writings and speeches convinced me I didn't belong in their camp. However, I discovered new perspectives on religion that shaped my understanding of reality.

Attending the Dallas UU church shaped my foundations. The preaching and my ongoing theological training confirmed that my beliefs and faith values weren't atypical, at least not within that community. My theological reframing slowly evolved through reflection and practice.

Being engaged in a UU community gave me the independence to consider my beliefs deeply. I did it without guilt or feeling I had betrayed my Christian upbringing. I realized it was proper to re-evaluate my faith perspectives, align my convictions with my experience, and embrace my current outlook as trustworthy. It was better to trust my intuition and take an authentic position versus retaining old beliefs no longer serving me nor registering as truth.

Going through the UU fellowship process forced me to clarify my beliefs more formally. I had to write my theology and its underpinnings for the Ministerial Fellowship Committee. Though not required to be an upstanding UU, it's inadvisable to skip this work. Consider it vitally important to your formation.

You'll discover it is a gift to yourself to develop a laser focus regarding your beliefs and faith convictions. Force yourself to work through this necessary aspect of UU faith identity. This is hard work. There are no shortcuts.

Write Out Your Core Convictions About Faith

This is an important use of time. Set aside quiet time to be clear about what you hold dear as convictions. You may have strong convictions about ethics, friendship, trust, love, family, God, the causes of suffering, community, etc. You may find such topics esoteric and of little value. Either way, you must know your core values and be able to articulate them; otherwise, it's hard to stand your ground. This helps me in life beyond UUism, too.

Jot Down Your Own Theology

You can accomplish this without training. All you need is time for thinking through your ideas. Here are a few areas for reflection. How did the world begin? Who is God? Why is there suffering? What is human nature? Are humans born with goodness? If not, what is the human impulse? These questions only scratch the surface of a comprehensive theology.

It helps to have exercises to get down to the full range of questions you need for reflection. The book titled *Articulating Your UU Faith* by Barbara Wells and Jaco B. Ten Hove is an excellent resource for working through this essential process.

Another outstanding book for shaping your thinking is Howard Stone and James Duke's book, *How to Think Theologically*. Their text breaks down theology into more traditional categories, which is helpful if you are a systematic thinker and desire a structured approach.

Stone and Duke provide a Christian orientation to thinking theologically, which is perfectly fine. You can adapt their work into a UU framework easily, but it takes time to think through their theological categories to find UU equivalents or make your own. Enlist your minister's help if you need another resource.

The list goes on and on regarding what to include in your theology or personal philosophy. You can amend it as you go along. As you grow in spirit, you need a foundation. Here is a resource for creating a personal theology.
I consider myself a spiritual humanist. It's not a category I've always claimed. I used to claim I was a mystical Christian. I'm likely to change again before it's all over.

Your Personal Mission Statement

Know your purpose in life and draft a personal mission statement. These need not be related to UUism, but both are essential for finding your way through UUA circles. There are benefits you haven't considered waiting for you. You'll better determine which ministries match your skills and gifts, which congregation to join, how to focus your community work, and which projects you'll enjoy.

My personal mission is encouraging UUs to become their best selves, live by expressing UU principles, and share the saving message of UUism with others they encounter along their path. A few years ago, I would have said my mission was helping people master their faith. I wrote a book about this. You can access it here. I've changed since then.

Learn To Relate With Non-UU Family and Friends

This may be the touchiest subject you'll face as a UU. How do you inform your family and friends that you are UU? How do you share the joy of your new faith? This is risky. Your family may abandon you when you announce your news. This is unavoidable when you act as an empowered human being. One might say it's a price you pay for being a UU.

Revealing yourself as UU to your family need not be cloaked in fear. Many new UUs live with a dreaded twist in their gut, expecting a harsh reaction from their family. (I know this because people have shared their stories with me.) They worry about whether to disclose at all. Others claim withholding their story protects people close to them from hurt and disappointment associated with knowing they've left the childhood faith. Adopting a courageous mindset is the best strategy for overcoming fear.

I suggest you speak up about your new faith as soon as you're able to comfortably and confidently describe UUism to others. You can then profess your UU values and principles honestly rather than slinking into the shadows. It's a perfect opportunity for a fierce conversation, a term coined by author Susan Scott. In her book, *Fierce Conversations*, Scott defines it as one "in which we come out from behind ourselves into the conversation and make it real. It's about moral courage, making requests, and taking action."

My family, mostly Christian[6], and I had a fierce conversation about my UU identity. They didn't flip out, have a heart attack, or die from the conversation.

To avoid surprising my wife, she and I discussed my plan for the upcoming dinner conversation with my family. I needed to be explicit with them about choosing a faith different from how I grew up. I needed to be honest, respectful, and not condescending about their beliefs.

The gathering presented no natural segue to the topic, so I started from scratch. When there was a natural pause, I jumped right in. They knew I was speaking to them because I spoke their names out loud.

I began the conversation by saying, "Mama and Tina, I need to share an important life change with you. You should know I have joined the Unitarian Universalist church. I no longer consider myself a Christian. I respect the way you've raised me, and I respect you as Christians, but I've chosen a different path."

---

6 *My father died before I became a UU. He practiced a staunch form of atheism, which I learned to appreciate from him as I got older. As a child, I didn't understand his passion against religion since everyone else around us was religious. As an adult, I realized his non-religious persona heavily influenced my ability to think critically about the Christian teachings that grounded much of my life.*

At first, they'd acted like they didn't hear me. My mother kept looking at her food. Then, my sister said something like "What?" I explained that it would not affect the love between us, but it was important for them to know about this aspect of my spiritual life.

My mother expressed no sentiment toward my breaking news. But she was conflict-avoidant, so it didn't surprise me. That is how the situation went down.

They later spoke with my wife about my decisions when I wasn't around, which was fine with me. I sensed they weren't on board but accepted it. We never spoke about my UU life person-to-person after that day. The anxiety reserved for that conversation ended up as wasted energy.

Expect To Lose Family and Friends

Some family members and friends will consider you a heretic, although they won't say it to your face. They won't know what to say, as with my family. But you know by their silence they have a new set of feelings toward you.

I've learned this from a variety of people. It's true for persons who choose atheism or humanism. Families have a strong culture or "family myths." Many families insist all members think and act alike. People with different beliefs end up ostracized. Such family culture is magnetic and only the strongest escape its force field.

Organizations such as Recovery from Religion can help people get through the aftermath of leaving the family faith. They'll recommend trained counselors in your area because quitting the family religion can cause an agonizing response. If you experience stress because of your family's reaction to you being a UU, seek professional help.

Friendship ties can be as strong as family. Most friends won't abandon your friendship, but some will act distantly toward you and show up less. Don't worry yourself sick and don't feel guilty or regretful because you were honest and open about your life. Anything else would have amounted to living a dishonest life with them and yourself.

A few of your deep friends will engage you in a conversation about your new beliefs. Try to be open about your choices and decisions. Don't get defensive about your faith perspective. Take the chance to answer their questions and queries with integrity as best you can.

First, if these friends (or family members) venture into your church with you, let's be honest. It isn't clear to many Blacks entering UU congregations that they've landed in a bona fide church[7]. They want to know if a church isn't Christian, what is it? That's the first question. Then why go to a place that resembles a church but feels less than a proper church? Those are proper questions Black people need UUs to answer.

The most important caveat is the "word." Where is the Bible? If it's missing, what do y'all preach from? You may need these questions answered yourself at this point. But increasingly, as a Black UU, you'll need to be able to answer these questions so people understand the distinctions. If you don't, it's on you that your family and friends don't get it and may not come to your new church. Learn and share the differences between how UU ministers use scripture compared to clergy in other traditions.

Expect To Gain Spiritual, Intellectual, and Social Freedom

Perhaps the biggest reward for identifying as UU is not hiding from your family. You become free. You can live with your well-being and UU identity secure. Not hiding in the shadows or masking your true values and beliefs from your friends and family provides you a level of independence easily underestimated if you're hiding.

You will feel a weight lifted from your shoulders. That's what I experienced after learning the value of transparency

---

7 The unusual nature of UU worship is striking not only to Blacks, but to other non-UUs. I've seen enough visitors leave service in the middle of worship to recognize when a person finds our services discomforting and not what they expected from a church.

and honesty. I was causing myself anguish and mental despair by hiding my needs. Here's a simple example.

I visited nursing homes, hospitals, and institutional living residences as a hospice chaplain. To get my job done, I had to ask the staff for help, but I resisted asking and snuck around the process. Finally, I had a "light bulb" moment and decided to stop avoiding people. Afterward, I lived transparently. Living openly as a UU versus sneaking around can offer you similar freedom.

I felt relief at once. It was night and day. I felt out in the open for something simple, but it made an enormous difference for my emotional and spiritual wellbeing.

The same thing happens when you reveal yourself as a UU to family and friends who think you are someone else other than who you are. You become free and liberated. It is hard explaining the sensation you experience by living free, but those who do it recognize what I'm talking about.

Joining a Long Tradition of Black Free Thought

Expressing yourself as a UU puts you within the rich, Black free thought movement. Many preceded you on your journey for a self-determined, value-driven life. They include Frederick Douglass, Lorraine Hansberry, Alice Walker, James Baldwin, and many other notable Black Americans. With this heritage, why worry about revealing yourself to others?

I recommend you read two notable texts to increase your appreciation for the Black free thought. Familiarizing yourself with this content will enhance your UU identity. Check out: *Black Freethinkers* by Christopher Cameron, and *Humanists in the Hood* by Sikivu Hutchison. Also listen to the Black Freethinkers podcast, which is full of woke and conscious conversations, albeit slightly more in-your-face.

STEP SIX

FINDING YOUR PEOPLE

Whether you are still "shopping" among Unitarian Universalist communities, or have found your home and joined a church, you have probably figured out who are potential kindred spirits there and who are likely not, or not yet. There may even be other Black members where you are, some of whom you may find affinity with. Beyond your chosen church, though, there are other ways to connect with Black UUs and other like-minded UUs, particularly online, and I cannot state strongly enough how healing those connections can be.

There are several Facebook groups dedicated to Black UU life. You need to be invited to the private groups by a member to gain access. Solid networking can help you find your way in. Here are a few to check out:

BLUU

Black Lives Unitarian Universalists (BLUU) is a Section 501(c)(3) non-profit based in St. Paul, Minnesota. Organized in 2015, its mission is supporting Black UUs and working for justice within Unitarian Universalism. Rev. Susan Frederick-Gray made a significant commitment to dismantling white supremacy culture within the UUA. As a part of that work, she spearheaded a campaign to raise $5 million for BLUU and the Black Lives Matter movement.

In June 2020, the UUA announced a partnership with BLUU. According to uua.org, the UUA will "partner with BLUU on their Havens and Harbors initiative to develop local nodes of Black communities within Unitarian Universalism. These groups will be woven into our system from the beginning. Harbors will receive covenanting community status within the UUA, and our staff will help support the congregations that host Harbors and Havens."

BLUU is a growing community for Black UUs. They host worship events, lead grassroots organizing, create courses, and offer social justice resources. Check out the website to see about BLUU's history, leadership, and programming.

DRUUMM

The organization DRUUMM (Diverse Revolutionary Unitarian Universalist Multicultural Ministries) is led by people of color. DRUUMM is a hub for Black UUs to connect

and organize. You'll meet other Blacks with similar interests and experiences mobilizing the faith.

DRUUMM hosts annual gatherings of its members. People network and share stories with one another, build solidarity, and create a beloved community. An important thing about

DRUUMM is your ability to meet seminarians and younger Black UUs. If you are a Black millennial, DRUUMM is a great outlet for you.

Finding Our Way Home

Finding Our Way Home is a community for UU religious professionals of color. The group gathers annually, and the event brings together ministers, seminarians, administrators, religious educators, musicians, and other UU religious professionals. They create community, fellowship, and retreat. UUs converge from throughout the country and meet for four days of programming.

FINDING OUR WAY HOME
Unitarian Universalist
Religious Professionals of Color

It makes you feel special as a UU of color. Our UUA president typically addresses the group along with other UUA dignitaries. The workshops are emotional, but filled with a spirit of love and have a UU of color worship flavor. We find empathy, comfort, and answers in a community that genuinely supports us. If you can attend a Finding Our Way Home experience, you're bound to find it supports your UU ministry and work.

Centering: Navigating Race, Authenticity, and Power in Ministry, **Mitra Rahnema, Editor**

Centering is an excellent collection of essays by BIPOC religious professionals sharing their experiences of working in Unitarian Universalism. It will open your eyes to authentic experiences within congregational and institutional life. This is a must-read.

REV. XOLANI KACELA, PH.D.

Widening the Circle of Concern: Report of the UUA Commission on Institutional Change, June 2020.

Widening the Circle of Concern is a report considered essential reading for all UUs. The CIC, led by the Rev. Leslie Takahashi, produced this thoughtful and transformation-inspiring work. In its own words, "the Unitarian Universalist Association (UUA) Commission on Institutional Change was established and charged by the UUA Board of Trustees to conduct an audit of white privilege and the structure of power within Unitarian Universalism, and analyze structural racism and white supremacy culture within the UUA. The Commission was in place for three years through the Virtual General Assembly in June of 2020." You can find this report, printed in paperback, on uua.org.

STEP SEVEN

FINDING A UU MENTOR

It's always a good idea to have a mentor. It's helpful if that person is Black. You can also benefit if the person is white, and you may find someone because of another identity you hold in common. Try making friends with a person who can help you navigate the way. Build a relationship with your mentor and pick their brain. Find out what they know about congregational life as a UU, particularly a Black UU.

Mentoring need not be formal. It can begin over coffee with someone more familiar with a community or UU life beyond a particular congregation. If that first coffee feels promising, build on it, and develop an even more trusting relationship.

Mentorship may be rooted in any number of goals on your part: Are you seeking some spiritual direction or help navigating from your old life and community to this new one? Are you interested in exploring leadership within the congregation, and want to learn from someone who's gone that route in your congregation or another? Are you interested in merging your spiritual and professional lives? Are you just looking for someone who's walked the walk you're on, whatever it may be? Depending on your goals, you might even suggest planning semi-regular meetings, at least for a while.

Learn Good Listening and Respond Accordingly

The key to a great mentor-protégé relationship is listening to your mentor and abiding by their advice as much as possible. Develop the capacity to trust what they've encouraged you to do. It may differ from what you would have done without them. You wouldn't need a mentor if you knew everything. Their advice may lead you in new directions. Be open and trust the process.

You may even become a mentor over time for another Black UU. It will be vitally important you steer them in the right direction. They'll depend on it to have a positive experience in the faith. Look ahead and imagine what you would want to offer your future protégé. Allow your imagination to help you navigate your current mentor-protégé arrangement. Make the most of this important relationship.

STEP EIGHT

LEARNING ABOUT UU
HISTORY & POLITY

M ake an honest effort to read UU history. There are tons of history books written on both the Unitarians and the Universalists. They are different in tone and complexity. Chances are your church has a library and there are several volumes available for check-out.

Some UU churches act as though they have no history. It's as if they spontaneously arrived in a vacuum with no past or tradition. Such an attitude will prevent you from discerning a sense of history and connectedness to the past. A quick Wikipedia version is often better than relying on local churches to teach UU history. Or pick up a book from InSpirit, the UUA book and gift store, like *Stirring the Nation's Heart: Eighteen Stories of Prophetic Unitarians and Universalists in the 19th Century* by Polly Peterson.

The most popular book on Black UU history is *Black Pioneers in a White Denomination* by Mark Morrison-Reed. It is accessible and beloved within UUism. You should read the book so you'll be well-versed in Black UU ancestry. The book illustrates that the UUA has a poor record of treating Black people fairly. Take this learning seriously so you have a more accurate understanding of what Black UUs have gone through. You stand on strong shoulders.

Learn your church's history after you've committed to

being there. It's good knowing where they came from and how they've changed. Study their covenants, which are agreements within a church. They help you navigate thorny situations, such as bad behavior and abuse of authority.

The bottom line is UUism represents a religious tradition. It is not a social group, social justice team, nor a freethought society. We have no connection with Unity Church. We are not the Universal Church that non-clergy join to perform weddings.

Though your UU place of worship may be a fellowship, society, or congregation, it is also a church. I hasten to point this out because many UUs don't acknowledge or accept that they are members of a religious organization. The religious movement, and your individual church, have histories.

What is Polity?

Polity is a fancy word describing how churches govern themselves. Churches have leadership levels that look like a business. Polity comprises the church's organizational chart and its rules. Keep in mind UUs don't have doctrine or creeds.

Robert's Rules of Order prevails within many UU churches. Committees and boards of trustees use them to structure meetings. These norms might be significant changes from your former church. Being aware of such differences helps you survive the UU world.

Polity differs by faith. Some denominations assign ministers to churches. Those ministers move from church to church when their leadership ability grows. Elders, such as bishops, decide where the ministers serve.

In the UU world, churches do not report to a governing body; they simply affiliate with the association. They are autonomous, or self-governing, and call their ministers on their own behalf. The "call" refers to the selection itself. There are always ministers in search of a church and vice versa. The UUA Ministerial Settlement System is our network for matching the two.

Churches create a search committee whose task is finding a minister. The committee spends a year or more in search. They create a packet they send to ministers. The ministers in search apply by submitting their packet to the search committee. A packet is a booklet detailing all facets of a congregation or clergyperson's ministry.

The committee interviews several ministers, judging whether their preaching inspires them and their skills match the congregation's needs. They narrow down the field to one minister, then invites that person for "candidating week." A church-wide vote on the minister ends the eight to nine-month process. The new minister starts in July or August. UUs refer to the new ministry as a settlement.

STEP NINE

GETTING INVOLVED BEYOND YOUR CONGREGATION

Learn About the UUA and Its Mission

Spend some time at uua.org. This will help you understand the larger framework in which UU congregations exist and develop their missions. This understanding will give you an advantage over UUs who don't know that the UUA (the headquarters office in Boston, MA) exists at all.

There's a reason some UUs wear those yellow Standing on the Side of Love T-shirts, march, and protest together at demonstrations. The book and gift store at the UU headquarters in Boston sells those shirts. Buy one and wear it proudly!

Volunteer Positions on Committees

The UUA has volunteer positions for its committees. The committees are at the regional and national levels. They make selections during the year and at General Assembly. Most require you to apply and compete for a spot. It's a great way to learn about the UUA, its mission, and how we do ministry. You need experience in a church and references as well. These committees need your Black voice. Take advantage of these opportunities for serving the UUA and learning what it means to be UU. Go to the website to find information about jobs and committee service.

What Is General Assembly?

Every year the UUA holds General Assembly (GA). It's an annual conference that attracts 2,500 to 5,000 UUs for a week of intense church work. During GA, delegates—people elected to represent their congregation—listen to proposals for Association-wide legislation, policy changes, rule changes, new initiatives and worship, hear a ton of updates, and spend time socializing.

What Happens There?

Representatives from the UUA headquarters, ministers, and laypersons deeply involved in the movement gather, and many speakers present contemporary ideas and give lectures to participants. GA lets you network with UUs from all walks of life. Travel to the event is self-funded, which leads attendance to be limited to retired people of means, ministers who have funds from their congregation, UUA staffers, and others who can pay for airfare, hotel, registration and food.

Scholarship Funds for BIPOCs

That being the reality, every year, the UUA sets aside funds for GA scholarships. Sometimes, the UUA funds travel and accommodations. For some recipients, it will waive registration fees, which can be several hundred dollars. The announcement for this scholarship fund usually begins at the end of March. Look for it on uua.org

Do Some Networking

GA is a great annual opportunity for immersion in UUA

and its initiatives. Plan your trip carefully because the pace is non-stop. You need to bring your best-extroverted self to make the most of it. You can make a ton of connections in a short time during the week.

Get Charged Up for Your Local Congregation

Take notes and share your knowledge when you return home. That's the only way people at the local level will know what happens at GA, unless they watch online. In most churches, people rarely focus on what happens beyond their walls. You can break that cycle by taking back what you've learned and get people fired up about broader UUA initiatives.

Considering Becoming a Religious Professional?

Are you interested in becoming a UU religious professional? Religious professionals include ministers, administrators, directors of religious education, musicians, finance professionals, and various jobs at the district, region, or national levels. This is not an all-inclusive listing.

For people seeking employment, it's important to know that the UUA hires people in both professional and support positions. Many jobs are remote. Once you establish yourself in the UUA world, check out those job listings. You may qualify for a position.

If you're interested in becoming a minister, review the requirements on the UUA website for ordained ministry (and read STEP 10 of this guide). To become a music director, hook up with a local UU musician or go to the AUUMM website. Review the credentialing requirements. To become a director of religious education, check out the LREDA website. There's also a resource for UU church administrators.

These careers require study and formal training. Often, you must pay for the coursework out of your pocket. Some congregations will sponsor you or pay for your tuition fees, but most will expect that you will do it yourself. Congregations rarely budget for members to become religious professionals. Some courses offer scholarships.

The cost of seminary education in the UUA world is expensive. You'll spend tens of thousands of dollars earning a Master of Divinity, or M.Div. degree. The process takes about three years. Directors of religious education arise from within the church itself and work their way up. They still need training, such as the LREDA Renaissance modules.

The UUA needs people of color in these positions. If you're interested, find someone in that field and discuss your aspirations with them. Once you have some goals, develop a mentorship with someone in the career field, create a path forward, and go for it.

STEP TEN

CONSIDERING MINISTRY

I've been in relationship with many Black UU clergy and know that most of us have struggled in this faith and in our ministries. Both clergy and laypersons who are Black are often living permanently in survival mode. This is simply stating the truth of the Black UU experience. There are times, though, when Black UU clergy hit a stride. Their ministries are dynamic, their churches are mission-focused, and they are helping people grow spiritually. They and their communities, together, are thriving.

That said, I have one Black UU non-clergy and two Black UU clergy colleagues whom I can rely on to answer the phone immediately when I call. That's not enough. There should be more. We need to build the number of Black ministers in the faith; there is strength in numbers. Being in ministry can be lonely, and you will need good relationships with both Black and non-Black colleagues and laity. However, I have adjusted my expectations regarding who will really be there for me. You will likely need to do the same.

Practical Matters

If you are (still) contemplating UU ministry, I applaud you! Graduating from seminary is hard. It is not for wimps.

Seminary faculty train you in ministry. But seminary admin types run the institutions like a business. They need income to ensure the institutions remain fiscally sustainable. Therefore, there are very few free rides or scholarships.

There are two accredited UU seminaries: Meadville Lombard Theological School in Chicago, Illinois, and Starr King School for the Ministry in Berkeley, California. Both offer the Master of Divinity (M. Div.) degree, which you need for ordained UU ministry. You can attend non-UU seminaries, too, then devise a plan to study UU history and polity on your own.

Keep in mind the M. Div. is a graduate degree, but it's not academic. It's called a professional degree. Most schools offer little scholarship money to theology students. You'll likely pay tuition out-of-pocket, which requires taking on debt. I love ministry but discourage you from assuming massive debt. It can take decades to repay.

There are no M. Div. school rankings. Don't equate finishing Harvard Divinity School with graduating from Harvard University. The undergraduate school ranks number one while the grad school has no rank. Finishing your program is what counts most. Don't get caught up with status. Focus on getting the most value for your money.

Most seminaries are related to a denomination and teach students to be religious leaders. A school such as Liberty University is very conservative (theologically and politically) but offers affordable tuition. Find a seminary offering you the best financial package while preparing you to be a competent UU minister. Your goal is passing the Ministerial Fellowship Committee (MFC). Where you got your M.Div. won't concern the committee.

Think deeply before embarking on seminary. You must be hungry for it because it is expensive, likely to leave you with debt, and the jobs awaiting you may not compensate you well enough to live as comfortably as you'd like while paying off your debt.

Ministering While Black

There is no doubt that I wouldn't be here as a solo UU parish minister without the mentoring, teaching, partnering, sharing, and love of many white ministerial colleagues. Some, such as Laurel Hallman, who invited me into the fold, and Sarah Lammert, who extended me a lifeline at a crucial time and embraced my spouse with love and care, have been indispensable and outstanding colleagues. My ace, Russell Elleven, is a true inspiration for many including myself. I believe more white colleagues can do "the work" of partnership and collaboration as these colleagues have.

The truth is that my experience working alongside white ministers has been mixed. I believe many white UU ministers would like to partner with Black UU ministers in the parish, but have trouble doing so as equals, whether they are conscious of that or not. I have served in the assistant minister chair in two large congregations. In both cases, the white colleagues were cordial and collaborative, but only to a point. Here are some key areas of contention.

White Colleagues May Not Understand
Black Preaching or Other Differences.

White UU preaching differs from Black preaching. The first affirms reason as primary. UU preachers rely heavily on the written word. Black preaching prizes: (1) scripture, (2) tradition, (3) reason, and (4) experience.[8]
These style differences lead to different results sometimes. They both provide hope and help people cope.

Black preaching depends upon emotional content and storytelling. UU clergy often disregard this. It happens so often that the UU scholar, Thandeka, teaches a course on preaching and emotion. Her work is based on her research on Schleiermacher, the famous theologian. She teaches UU

8 This is known in Methodism as the Wesleyan Quadrilateral. However, it is largely adapted by many Black preaching theorists. The emphasis in most traditions begins with experience.

clergy to access the emotional part of their minds, their personal narratives, and humor. The combination rouses the UU worship experience.

Many Black UU clergy grow up hearing this preaching style and can access this emotion easily. There are exceptions. I'll admit I am one who has to work on this area. But one way or another, Black clergy who integrate their authentic style may experience a backlash from white UU supervisors. I've seen white colleagues showing their second-hand shame because of my preaching style.

White and Black Clergy Collegiality

UU ministry teams mirror society. White ministers usually supervise Black ministers. Most churches won't set it up the other way. The white person will contribute to the Black person's success by accepting the Black person's style. Then they must advocate for them through all circumstances[9]. When the white minister disagrees with the Black colleague or vice versa, they should keep their lines of communication open and hash out the differences. The white person needs to give in sometimes and not have to win every situation.

Problems arise when, for instance, white church members find fault with the Black colleague and the white supervisor goes along with it. It's especially problematic when the white supervisor assumes the white church member is automatically more credible than the Black clergy person and demands the Black person defend what happened. It's happened to me at both large churches I've been part of. And, as you no doubt know, it's happened to any number of Black people, particularly Black people in authority, in any number of settings.

9 I practice this with church staff, too. All my staff knows I'm in their corner from jump street. I don't tolerate parishioners marginalizing staff in any way. Nor do I side with parishioners against staff. I expect parishioners to speak directly with staff and resolve differences. Likewise, staff knows they work for me, the minister, not volunteers. I believe this creates healthy boundaries for parishioners and staff and prevents members from showing up demanding staff resources.

In the UU church setting, such situations demand that we ask: what happened to our collegiality? Don't call a person your colleague if you're going to treat them otherwise. Colleagues should stand by one another. Colleagues who stand with a church member against another colleague, without consulting the colleague first, are violating covenant. They should be held accountable by the UUMA. Black UU clergy who find themselves in such situations should immediately reach out to a good officers rep for help and support.

The white colleague who insists on correcting "deficiencies" dooms the relationship. Black clergy should be ready for this. You'll need an excellent mentor who can help you navigate these rough waters.

The white colleague needs to understand that differences are real but not necessarily better or worse. Get on board with differences, be able to talk about it, and stand up to parishioners who are primed and ready to complain about the Black clergy to white clergy. Don't ask the Black clergy to defend themselves. Don't resort to white supremacy tactics. Be a partner.

FOR ALLIES (INCLUDING CLERGY):

It would be a mistake approaching this content as a white reader, intent on discrediting what you read. Try not to respond, "I don't understand how he sees race in that!"

Your ability to perceive unconscious bias, racism, or micro-aggressions directed toward Black UUs and Black clergy colleagues should grow by reading this. Think of "deficiencies" or just different ways of doing things you may have exhibited over the years and how often they have been allowed, otherwise met with patience, or ignored, rather than leapt on and attacked. That is white privilege.

A persistent inability to understand what I share here does not erase nor detract from the observable and verifiable facts of Black people's lives. That you can't see those dynamics, to the point of denying their existence, is why such bias is called "unconscious." Your job is to raise it to the conscious level, work to recognize it in yourself and others, and equip yourself to better support Black colleagues and other Black people in your community and beyond.

UU Clergy Are Not Trained In Supervision and Conflict Resolution

Divinity schools do not train UU clergy to supervise. Nor do they teach seminarians social skills. Many white UU ministers rely on personality and position to supervise Black assistant ministers. This works until the Black minister shows up as their fully human self, in a way that takes a white minister by surprise. Both ministers must *keep it 100* for a genuine relationship. If the white minister brings their whole self but gets angry and hostile when the Black person does the same, that's simply unjust.My experience shows that white colleagues (and churchgoers) find it burdensome serving alongside a Black person. We begin working as a team. Then the white minister slips into resentment when I express my UU ideas, which may differ some from mainstream (white) UU notions. One would think my ideas are equally valid, given my experience and education. I have two business degrees and tons of corporate, government, and military experience, experience as a minister and best practices under my belt. My skill set is deep.

During my career in ministry, I have had white UU colleagues stop talking to me when I revealed my full self. They cut collegiality, except when we had to work together. Their internalized white superiority ruined our relationship.

Rather than work through differences, compromise, and change, white colleagues too often dispose of Black colleagues. This is a dynamic not unique to the ministry, but common in middle and upper management elsewhere (or even lower on the hierarchy when a Black employee begins to show promise or speaks up). Just like their counterparts in other arenas, white ministers may use the board or their positional power to end the Black clergy's contract. A white colleague excused me under false pretenses only to replace me with a white non-clergy, non-UU person. A white UU clergy later replaced that person. Hence, my departure marked a circuitous replacement of a Black clergy person with a white clergy person.

Another white colleague canned me after months of outright deception by that same colleague only to see the colleague replace me with a less experienced, Black seminarian whom the colleague "liked" more, but who was not offered positional authority that might allow him to hold the white colleague accountable. Yet another white colleague once offered me a co-ministry, then "went dark" when I asked for a fair salary and equal stature.

Each of these situations reflects white supremacy culture in UU ministry. Only the ministers in charge can change the culture by recognizing the dynamic, understanding just how common it is, taking responsibility, and getting to the other side of the discomfort they feel in partnering with Black clergy.

When white and Black clergy co-minister, they need an agreement that casts the Black and white clergy's status and importance as equal. The two must then work out their differences on behalf of the congregation's mission. They (and perhaps also the church board) must also agree not to rush to dismiss the Black clergy when things are hard.

There Are Very Few Clergy Invitations To Preach

I seldomly receive invitations to preach at white UU colleagues' churches. Black clergy invite each other to preach. I can count on one hand how many invitations I've received from white colleagues. (It was different in Texas where all my colleagues invited me to preach.) It seems to go against the culture for UU colleagues to open their pulpit.

I'm unaware of why my white colleagues don't invite me to preach. Maybe I'm perceived as a poor preacher. It could be they don't invite anyone to preach. Maybe their congregations don't allow them to have guest preachers. Could they lack money for an honorarium? I doubt that. Some have the mindset that only they can preach what their congregation needs to hear.

The lacking relations between white and Black clergy mirror the lacking Black people in UU pews. One can understand how UU churches appear unfriendly to potential Black parishioners. Black members and visitors may say nothing, but they're able to observe and detect these behaviors. Collaborating establishes trust between colleagues, and not pursuing collaboration is a missed opportunity for building bridges. More shared pulpits between white and Black ministers would model for churchgoers a way to break down the color barrier in the UU church and their own lives.

A Parting Caveat

It is important that Black ministers (and BIPOCs in general) share our experiences. Such sharing helps us feel less alone. It helps us understand the pressures of this work and adjust our expectations of white peers. I am not bashing my white peers or grinding an ax by naming these observations. There is plenty of room to examine how white UU ministers lead and supervise, particularly when Black colleagues are in the mix. UUism will only reach its full potential when white ministers work on dismantling white supremacy culture behind the scenes. White UU clergy must share power with non-white clergy to truly build the beloved community. As Dr. King said, that will "require a qualitative change in our souls" and in our lives.

A LAST WORD TO ASPIRING ALLIES

I'm not arguing you should accept this content as "the gospel" or that my views apply to all Black UUs. I'm merely saying keeping it 100 in this context is about accepting Black experience as told by Black people as valid, factual, and experiential without disputing it. It's likely that a white ally reading this content will respond by attempting to validate it with other Black UUs, which is fine and expected. Those persons may validate my experience. They may even provide more insight. I hope that is the case. But in the event that you have no Black UU members or friends in your UU church, or even if one Black friend says this hasn't been their experience, don't be in a hurry to discount this content. Don't be tempted to categorize it as invalid or appearing unsubstantiated because you've not experienced it nor has anyone approached you directly with this type of critique. Take seriously what you read here as grounds and evidence of genuine experience. Don't discount what I've written nor grow defensive about the critiques I've presented. Just take it at face value as being the experience of many Black UUs. Think on it. Try to imagine being us. Let it change you and how you relate.

That's keeping it 100.

ABOUT THE AUTHOR

Xolani "XK" Kacela, Ph.D. serves as the Minister of the Unitarian Universalist Church of Las Cruces, New Mexico. The church welcomes all people and has the motto: "May we convey love in all we do." He has served in UU churches in Dallas, TX, and Durham, NC. He has also served as a hospice and hospital chaplain before entering parish ministry.

XK also currently serves as a chaplain in the New Mexico Air National Guard, based in Albuquerque, NM. Before that, he'd served with the District of Columbia National Guard at Joint Base Andrews, MD, and worked at U.S. Special Operations Command at MacDill Air Force Base in Tampa, FL. He also developed and taught chaplaincy-related curricula at the Joint Special Operations University at MacDill Air Force Base, FL. He began his military career with the Texas Air National Guard in Ft. Worth, TX. He has deployed four times, including service during the war in Iraq.

XK enjoys many hobbies. His favorite pastime is hanging out with his wife, Tamara. They could make their own outdoor reality show. They're always looking for the next adventure. You can catch them ice fishing, bow fishing, and hunting deer, javelina, and oryx.

You can listen to XK's weekly radio show, Take On

Faith, on lccommunityradio.org. The program airs live on Saturdays at 10 am MT. Each episode features a guest with a unique faith perspective.

Check out his publishing website: revdrxk.com or his blog, revdrxk.com/blog. He has written five books, including a memoir and three children's books. Also, be sure to read the interview with the author.

You can find XK's other writings on his other website, MasteringYourOwnFaith.com, and you can reach him at xk@revdrxk.com.

Connect with XK:
Follow XK on Twitter:
https://twitter.com/XolaniKacela

Friend XK on Facebook:
https://www.facebook.com/revdrxk

Follow XK on YouTube:
https://www.youtube.com/xolanikacela

Made in the USA
Las Vegas, NV
27 June 2022

50770767R10050